HITS, HANKIES, AND HOMERS

THE STORY OF
THE MINNESOTA TWINS

Stew Thornley

Lerner Publications Company / Minneapolis

Lerner Publications Company
A division of Lerner Publishing Group
241 First Avenue North
Minneapolis, MN 55401 U.S.A.

Website address: www.lernerbooks.com

Cover and text designed by Steven Foley.
All photos courtesy of the Minnesota Twins.
Cover photo by Richard Orndorf.

Library of Congress Cataloging-in-Publication Data

Thornley, Stew.
    Hits, hankies, and homers: the story of the Minnesota Twins / by Stew
Thornley.
       p.   cm.
    Includes index.
    ISBN 0-8225-3699-4 (pbk. : alk. paper)
    1. Minnesota Twins (Baseball team)—History—Juvenile
literature. [1. Minnesota Twins (Baseball team)—History.
2. Baseball—History.] I. Title.
GV875.M55 T56   2000
796.357'64'09776579—dc21   00-009364

Manufactured in the United States of America
1 2 3 4 5 6 -JR- 05 04 03 02 01 00

Some of the Twins greatest stars model the various team uniforms. Left to right: *Harmon Killebrew, Tony Oliva, Chuck Knoblauch, Paul Molitor, Kent Hrbek, and Bert Blyleven*

Table of Contents

Eric Milton pitched a no-hitter against the Anaheim Angels in September 1999.

Major-League Excitement

Eric Milton kicks and fires. The batter, Jeff DaVanon, swings so hard that he nearly digs himself into the ground. He misses.

The fans in the Metrodome are on their feet. It's a late-season contest between the Minnesota Twins and the Anaheim Angels in September 1999. Not much is at stake with the outcome of the game. But Twins left-hander Eric Milton is on the verge of something very special. He's just one strike away from a no-hitter.

Milton delivers a ball high and outside, but his next pitch is on target. DaVanon swings and misses again. Milton shakes his fist in celebration. The crowd erupts. Fans elsewhere in Minnesota get the news from Herb Carneal, the Twins longtime announcer. "Swing and a miss! He struck him out," Carneal calls out to his many radio listeners. "A no-hit, no-run game for Eric Milton!"

It's all part of the excitement of Twins baseball.

For nearly 40 years, major-league baseball has been a big part of life in Minnesota. The Minnesota Twins have provided thrills for residents of the state, as well as for fans throughout the Upper Midwest. Through the years, the Twins have given fans the chance to see many baseball greats. The stars have included Harmon Killebrew, Tony Oliva, Rod Carew, and Kirby Puckett for the Twins. Opposing players like Mickey Mantle, Hank Aaron, Cal Ripken, Mark McGwire, and Ken Griffey Jr. have also played here.

The Twins have been a summertime tradition, providing memories for generations of fans. Many people who attended games at Metropolitan Stadium with their parents bring their own kids to Twins games at the Metrodome.

But the area had a rich baseball heritage even before the Twins arrived. Amateur and semi-professional teams were the pride of small towns in the Upper Midwest. Minor-league teams flourished in many cities. The most notable were the Minneapolis Millers and the St. Paul Saints, who had a fierce rivalry dating back to the 1880s.

For many years, the Millers played at Nicollet Park in Minneapolis. It was a cozy but rickety ballpark that was falling apart by the 1950s. In 1956 the

The original Minnesota Twins. The team won only 70 games in 1961, but it quickly improved.

6

Calvin Griffith, who passed away in 1999, brought major-league baseball to Minnesota in 1961.

Millers got a new place to play: Metropolitan Stadium, a gleaming, triple-decked facility in the suburb of Bloomington. But those behind the construction of the stadium had more than the Millers in mind. They hoped the new ballpark would help lure a major-league team to Minnesota. Within a few years, it had.

In late 1960, Calvin Griffith, owner of the Washington Senators, announced that he was moving his American League team.

Major-league baseball was coming to Minnesota.

Metropolitan Stadium was the home of the Twins from 1961 to 1981. Among the team's early stars were Harmon Killebrew (left inset), *who hit more than 40 home runs in a season eight times in his career, and Bob Allison* (middle inset), *another powerful slugger in the Twins lineup in the 1960s. Jim Kaat* (right inset), *a pitcher who joined the team in 1961, would end his career as a Twin with 189 wins, the most in team history.*

A Good Start in Minnesota

Minnesotans were excited about their Twins. "Win Twins!" bumper stickers decorated cars around the state. Baseball was the hot topic of conversation just about everywhere. People tuned into Twins games on the radio while they went about their summertime activities. And more than 1.2 million fans flocked to Met Stadium during the Twins first season in 1961.

The team that came to Minnesota in 1961 wasn't a powerhouse, though. The Senators had often finished last in their years in Washington. Still, the new Minnesota Twins had some great players. Harmon Killebrew had hit 42 home runs with the Senators in 1959 and would top that total many times in Minnesota. He had a slugging teammate in Bob Allison, the American League Rookie of the Year in 1959.

The Twins won only 70 games and lost 90 in 1961, but they moved up in the standings in the coming years. With Sam Mele as manager, Minnesota finished second to the mighty New York Yankees in 1962. Killebrew led the league with 48 home runs that year, but the highlight of the season came on

Tony Oliva won batting titles in his first two full seasons in the majors. Each time, American League president Joe Cronin (right) gave him a silver bat.

Sunday, August 26. Southpaw Jack Kralick took the mound against the Kansas City Athletics and began mowing down the hitters. Going into the ninth inning, Kralick not only held the A's hitless but he also hadn't allowed a single base runner. He was on the verge of a perfect game, one of the rarest events in baseball. With one out in the ninth, though, Kralick walked George Alusik. His perfect game was gone, but he retired the final two batters and finished with a no-hitter.

The Twins had another good year in 1963 but suffered a setback the following season. Even though Harmon Killebrew hit 49 home runs and Tony Oliva led the American League in batting average and was named the league's Rookie of the Year, the team ended the 1964 season in a tie for sixth place. It was a disappointing year, but the Twins bounced back.

In July 1965, Minnesota hosted the All-Star Game. The event brought national attention to the state, but there was more excitement to come

Because of an injury, Killebrew missed part of the season and hit only 25 home runs. But others picked up the slack. Tony Oliva won the batting title again. Jim "Mudcat" Grant had a great year on the mound, winning 21 games.

The real star of the season was shortstop Zoilo Versalles. He was terrific at the plate, with a batting average of .273 and 19 home runs. As the team's lead-off hitter, Versalles gave the Twins the spark they needed to win the American League pennant. Ending the long dynasty of the New York Yankees, the Twins had won a spot in the 1965 World Series.

Their opponents were the Los Angeles Dodgers, who had a superb pitching staff led by Don Drysdale and Sandy Koufax. The Twins surprised the Dodgers by defeating Drysdale, then Koufax, in the first two games of the

The Twins celebrate after clinching the American League pennant in 1965. That season Zoilo Versalles (inset) *won the American League Most Valuable Player award.*

Mudcat Grant (left) won 21 games during the regular season in 1965 and 2 more in the World Series. Jim Perry (left, facing page) was the first Twins pitcher to win the Cy Young Award. Rod Carew (right, facing page) was the American League Rookie of the Year in 1967. Two years later, Carew won his first of seven American League batting titles.

series. But the Dodgers came back with three wins in a row. In the sixth game, Mudcat Grant kept the Twins alive. He pitched a six-hitter and hit a three-run homer, leading the Twins to a 5-1 win and forcing a seventh game. Sandy Koufax was too much for Minnesota in the finale, though. He pitched a three-hit shutout and beat the Twins 2-0 to win the World Series for Los Angeles.

The Twins finished second the next year, with the help of a 25-game-winning season from Jim Kaat. The team's members then found themselves in a tremendous pennant race in 1967, battling down to the wire with the Boston Red Sox and the Detroit Tigers. The season ended with a weekend series in Boston. Minnesota needed to win at least one of the two games, but Boston won both games, and the Red Sox, not the Twins, went to the World Series.

After a seventh-place finish in 1968, the Twins were primed for a good year in 1969. Both leagues had expanded to 12 teams and were split into divisions. The Twins had a new manager, fiery Billy Martin, and "Martin's Marauders" gave fans a season to remember. Rod Carew and Cesar Tovar created havoc on the base paths. Tovar set a team record with 45 stolen bases, and Carew stole 19, including 7 steals of home. Carew—who had been the American League Rookie of the Year two years before—also won the batting title in 1969. Tony Oliva had a great season, knocking in more than 100 runs for the first

time in his career. On the mound, Jim Perry and Dave Boswell both won 20 games. But the season belonged to Harmon Killebrew. He hit 49 home runs and drove in 140, leading the majors in both categories. Killebrew was named the Most Valuable Player in the American League.

The Twins were good, but they went up against an even better team, the Baltimore Orioles, in the American League play-offs. The Orioles swept the play-off series to eliminate the Twins.

The Twins fired Billy Martin after the 1969 season, even though he'd led the team to first place in the West Division. With Bill Rigney as the new manager, the Twins won the West again in 1970. Killebrew had another big year, homering 41 times. Jim Perry won 24 games and became the first Minnesota pitcher to win the Cy Young Award. Rookie Bert Blyleven, still a teenager, came up from the minors and won 10 games. But once again the Twins couldn't handle Baltimore in the play-offs. They were swept for the second straight year.

The Minnesota Twins first decade had offered a lot of great moments. There would be many more, but there would also be some rough spots in between.

Harmon Killebrew hit the 500th home run of his career in 1971. He finished his career with 573 home runs, fifth on the all-time home run list.

Downs and Ups

The Twins had more downs than ups in 1971. Tony Oliva was on fire with the bat, slugging the ball to all fields, but he suffered a serious knee injury in Oakland in late June. He still managed to win the batting title for the third time, but he was never the same player after the injury.

In August Killebrew hit the 500th home run of his career. He finished the season with 119 runs batted in (RBIs), but his home run total dropped to 28. As a team, the Twins dropped even more. They finished in fifth place, 25$\frac{1}{2}$ games out of first. For the first time in team history, the Twins failed to top the million mark in attendance.

The season began a dry spell for the Twins. They still had some fine players, especially second baseman Rod Carew. After struggling to recover from a knee injury in 1971, he bounced back in 1972, starting a string of four consecutive batting titles. Nevertheless, the team still had trouble winning more games than it lost during those years.

The Twins hired a new manager, Gene Mauch, in 1976. At first the change didn't seem to make much difference. The Twins got off to a slow start but came on strong in the second half of the season. They rose to third place and finished just five games out of first.

The strong finish gave the Twins hope for the future. It also set the stage for an exciting year in 1977, one that brought the fans swarming back to Met Stadium. With a powerful batch of hitters, the team was known as the "Lumber Company." Larry Hisle led the American League in RBIs. Lyman Bostock hit .336 and scored 104 runs. Glenn Adams did some heavy hitting and set a Twins record in late June by driving in eight runs in one game.

Adams was actually upstaged by Rod Carew in that game, one of the most memorable in Twins history. A crowd of more than 46,000 filled Met Stadium to see the Twins battle the Chicago White Sox for the top spot in the West Division. Carew scored five runs and drove in six as the Twins outslugged Chicago, 19-12, to move past the Sox into first place. He ended the season with a batting average of .388, the best in the majors in 20 years.

Larry Hisle led the American League with 119 RBIs in 1977, while Lyman Bostock hit .323 in 1976 and .336 in 1977.

Dave Goltz never had a losing season in a Minnesota uniform.

On the mound, Dave Goltz, a strong right-hander and a Minnesota native, won 20 games. Another Minnesota-born pitcher, Tom Johnson, won 16 games, all in relief. The excitement was back at the Met, and the Twins drew more than a million fans for the first time since 1970. The team stayed in the pennant hunt before tailing off in the final month of the season.

More disturbing than the late-season swoon was the prospect of the Twins losing some of their stars. Players were now allowed to sign with new teams after their contracts expired, and Calvin Griffith didn't have enough money to compete with other owners in the free-agent market.

Hisle and Bostock, two of the team's big guns, signed with new teams for the 1978 season. Without them, the offense sputtered. Rod Carew won his

Kent Hrbek hit a home run in his first major-league game with the Twins in 1981 and many more after that in his 14-year career with Minnesota.

seventh American League batting title in 1978, but he, too, appeared to be on his way out. Rather than risk losing him to free agency, Griffith traded Carew to the California Angels before the 1979 season. The Lumber Company had been dismantled.

The Twins still fought hard in 1979, and they stayed in the race for the West Division title until the final week of the season. After that they dropped back again, floundering during the next two years before small crowds at Met Stadium.

Even though the 1981 season was largely a dismal one, some newcomers provided a boost near the end of the year. Kent Hrbek, who had grown up close to Met Stadium, joined the team in August. He played his first game at Yankee Stadium and won it for the Twins with a home run in the twelfth inning. Over the next month, two more players broke in with a bang. Tim Laudner and Gary Gaetti both homered in their first games.

The end of an era came on a drizzly afternoon on the last day of September. The Twins lost to the Kansas City Royals in the final baseball game held at Met Stadium. A new domed stadium was about to open on the edge of downtown Minneapolis.

Minnesota finished the season with the worst record in the American League West. But a new stadium—and new hopes—were awaiting the Twins and their fans in Minneapolis.

The Metrodome became the Twins new home in 1982. Gary Gaetti (left) helped the Twins win their first World Series five years later.

Joining the Twins in 1984, Kirby Puckett later won the American League batting title in 1989 and led the league in RBIs in 1994. An eye disease forced him to retire in 1996.

A Whole New Ball Game

Rain-outs became a thing of the past for Minnesota in 1982. Whatever the weather, games could always go on inside the Hubert H. Humphrey Metrodome. The first game—an exhibition contest—took place on a cold Saturday night in early April. Kent Hrbek hit the first two home runs in the new stadium. A few days later, Dave Engle hit the Metrodome's first regular-season home run as the Twins opened the season with a loss to the Seattle Mariners. Many more losses followed, but so did lots of excitement.

In a lineup loaded with young players, Kent Hrbek led the way. He had a 23-game hitting streak that extended into May. That same month, the Twins acquired 21-year-old slugger Tom Brunansky in a trade. Gaetti and Laudner also contributed, along with a new pitcher, Frank Viola. The rookies couldn't keep the Twins from losing more than 100 games—the most losses in team history—but the newcomers gave fans a reason to believe that better times lay ahead.

Kirby Puckett joined the Twins in May 1984 and got four hits in his first game. With his hustle and enthusiastic style of play, he immediately became a fan favorite. Also in 1984, Carl Pohlad purchased the team from Calvin Griffith. Soon after that, the Twins caught fire and moved to the top of the West Division standings. With only a week left in the season, they held first place, but they lost their last six games and finished in a tie for second.

Fans were optimistic after the good season, but their hopes were squelched a bit as the Twins struggled during the next two years. What came next, however, was unforgettable.

Key members of the 1987 championship team, left to right: *Gary Gaetti, Tom Brunansky, Kirby Puckett, Kent Hrbek, and Roy Smalley*

Tom Kelly (left) *played for the Twins in 1975 and coached the team before taking over as manager in September 1986. Carl Pohlad* (above) *bought the Twins in 1984 and has since seen the team win the World Series twice.*

The Twins had a new look in 1987, with new logos and a different design on their uniforms. They also had Tom Kelly, starting his first full season as manager. Finally, they had a top relief pitcher, Jeff Reardon, acquired in a trade with Montreal.

While the new faces helped, it was the old ones—Hrbek, Puckett, Gaetti, and Brunansky—who fueled the surge that brought the Twins to the top in 1987. They moved into first place and stayed there over most of the season's second half. Puckett had a lot of big games, but none bigger than the one held on August 30 in Milwaukee. Against the Brewers, Puckett had six hits, capping the day with his second home run of the game.

The Twins went on to win the West, but few people outside Minnesota thought they'd have much of a chance against Detroit in the league play-offs.

With his hard-nosed style of play, Dan Gladden was a favorite of Metrodome fans. He hit a grand slam in the first game of the 1987 World Series and scored the winning run in the seventh game of the 1991 World Series.

The Twins thought otherwise and surprised the Tigers. They won the play-off series four games to one.

The final game was held in Detroit on a Monday afternoon. That night, the Twins came back to the Metrodome. Screaming fans packed the stadium—not to watch a game but to salute the team.

The players were overwhelmed by the fan support, which continued in the World Series against St. Louis. Waving "homer hankies" and producing enormous noise levels with their cheering, the fans helped propel the Twins to wins in the first two games. Dan Gladden hit a grand slam in the series opener, and Bert Blyleven pitched a strong game the next night.

Minnesota then lost three games in St. Louis. Back in the Metrodome for Game Six, they fell behind and things looked bleak.

But the team—and the fans—wouldn't give up. Don Baylor tied the game with a two-run homer in the fifth. The next inning, the Twins took the lead on a run-scoring single by Steve Lombardozzi. Then Kent Hrbek iced the game by unloading a grand slam.

Ace Frank Viola pitched the seventh game for Minnesota. He gave up two runs in the second but shut the Cardinals down after that. The Twins scored in the second and fifth innings to tie the game. They took the lead in the sixth on Greg Gagne's bases-loaded infield single and added an insurance run in the eighth.

Reardon came in to get the final three outs. When St. Louis's Willie McGee grounded out to end the game—and the World Series—the Metrodome erupted.

Players and fans had kept the faith the entire season—even when no one else believed in them. The Twins were world champions.

Tim Laudner picks up Jeff Reardon after the final out of the 1987 World Series. For the first time, the Twins were world champions.

Frank Viola was the Most Valuable Player of the 1987 World Series. The next year, he won 24 games and the Cy Young Award.

The Tradition Continues

Minnesota didn't repeat in 1988, but it did have the American League's best pitcher in Frank Viola. The southpaw won 24 games and received the Cy Young Award.

The Twins dropped further in the standings over the next two years, all the way to last place in 1990. Throughout the Twins history, though, big seasons had followed disappointing ones. By June 1991, the team had heated up. A 15-game winning streak—the longest in team history—put Minnesota in first place.

Scott Erickson was magnificent on the mound. He won 12 consecutive games, including 2 shutouts in a row, during the first half of the year. He finished with 20 wins. Not far behind was Jack Morris with 19 wins. A native of St. Paul, Morris was playing his first season with the Twins after many fine years with Detroit.

Another newcomer was rookie Chuck Knoblauch, who played a sterling second base and also sparkled on offense. Veterans like Hrbek and Puckett produced their usual heroics, and the Twins won the West Division by eight games.

After finishing off the Toronto Blue Jays in five games in the league play-offs, the Twins moved on to the World Series. Their opponents were the Atlanta Braves, another team that had finished in last place the year before.

That World Series was one of the most spectacular ever played. Jack Morris took the mound in the first game, pitching well and helping the Twins win. In the second game, Scott Leius broke a 2–2 tie in the last of the eighth with a home run off Atlanta's Tom Glavine. Rick Aguilera closed out the game in the ninth, giving the Twins a two-games-to-none lead.

In Atlanta the Twins lost a pair of close games, then got trounced in Game Five to fall behind in the series. It was a familiar World Series pattern for the Twins—win the first two at home and then lose three on the road.

The Twins came back to the Metrodome needing a win to prolong the series. They were up to the challenge, especially Kirby Puckett. In the third inning, with a runner on first, Atlanta's Ron Gant hit a long drive to left-center field. Puckett got to the wall, timed his leap, and sprung high in the air. He snared the ball with an outstretched glove, robbing Gant with a dazzling catch and killing a rally.

The game went into extra innings. Puckett came to the plate to start the last of the eleventh. He turned on a pitch and drove it deep to left-center. It settled into

Jack Morris's (left) one season with the Twins, 1991, was a great one. He had 19 wins in the regular season and 2 in the World Series (including a 10-inning shutout) and was named the World Series Most Valuable Player. Kirby Puckett (right) was the star of the sixth game of the 1991 World Series. He made a great catch early on and finished the game with a home run in the eleventh inning.

the stands for a game-winning home run, sending the series to a seventh game.

In the finale, Morris pitched for the Twins against John Smoltz of Atlanta. It was a classic duel, and the game was scoreless into the eighth. The Braves looked to break it open when they put runners on second and third with no outs. But Gant grounded out feebly with the runners holding. After an intentional walk, the Twins turned a double play to get out of the inning.

Minnesota loaded the bases with one out in the last of the eighth, but Kent Hrbek hit a soft liner that turned into a double play. The game stayed scoreless into extra innings. Jack Morris was still on the mound, and he put the Braves down in order in the top of the tenth. In the bottom of the inning, Dan Gladden led off with a double. Chuck Knoblauch laid down a sacrifice bunt, sending Gladden to third. After Puckett and Hrbek were intentionally walked, Gene Larkin pinch-hit for Jarvis Brown.

Larkin connected on the first pitch and sent a drive to left that dropped behind the outfielders. Gladden held at third until he could see the ball wouldn't be caught. He then trotted home, where jubilant teammates awaited him. For the second time in five seasons, the Twins were champions of the baseball world.

It looked like the team might repeat in 1992. The Twins played well and held a three-game lead over the Oakland Athletics in late July. Then the A's came to the Metrodome and swept three games from Minnesota. It was a turning point for the Twins. They finished second to Oakland in the West Division and have yet to return to the top.

While the team struggled through the rest of the 1990s, individual players provided many highlights. Dave Winfield, who grew up playing baseball on the sandlots of St. Paul, came to the Twins in 1993 after many good years with San Diego, the New York Yankees, and California. In September 1993, Winfield got the 3,000th hit of his career. A few years later, another St. Paul native, Paul Molitor, joined the Twins to finish out his Hall of Fame career. Molitor got his 3,000th hit in 1996.

A sad moment came for the Twins during spring training in 1996. Kirby Puckett, coming off an outstanding year, began having vision problems. He was diagnosed with the eye disease glaucoma, which brought his career to a premature halt. In 1997 the Twins held a memorable weekend event to honor Puckett and to retire his number, 34. Puckett has since moved into the front office and works as a vice president for the Twins. He also serves as an instructor for individual players and for the Twins minor-league teams.

Just as Calvin Griffith had been plagued by rising salaries in the 1970s, the Twins again had difficulties competing with some of the richer teams for top players. Even so, the Twins developed a number of fine young players, such as Brad Radke. In 1997 the right-hander won 20 games for Minnesota, including a stretch of 12 wins in a row.

The 1999 season was marked by the emergence of many rookies. Shortstop Cristian Guzman, third baseman Corey Koskie, and outfielders Jacque Jones and Torii Hunter were among the newcomers who joined dependable veterans like Ron Coomer and Matt Lawton.

Radke led the mound staff, which included young pitchers such as Joe Mays, LaTroy Hawkins, and Eric Milton. Milton topped off the 1990s with his huge no-hitter against the Angels in mid-September.

Even with the youngsters performing well, the Twins finished in last place in 1999. But then again, they had done that in 1990, and the fans will never forget what happened next.

And Minnesota fans will never forget all the thrills they've had from major-league baseball over the first 40 years. And they will never stop hoping for great things in the future.

Brad Radke, who was drafted by the Twins in 1991 and joined the majors in 1995, won 20 games in 1997 and led the club in wins in 1998 and 1999.

Selected Twins Stats

Retired Numbers
3:   Harmon Killebrew
6:   Tony Oliva
14: Kent Hrbek
29: Rod Carew
34: Kirby Puckett
42: Jackie Robinson*

Kirby Puckett

League Leaders in Batting Average
1964: Tony Oliva, .323
1965: Tony Oliva, .321
1969: Rod Carew, .332
1971: Tony Oliva, .337
1972: Rod Carew, .318
1973: Rod Carew, .350
1974: Rod Carew, .364
1975: Rod Carew, .359
1977: Rod Carew, .388
1978: Rod Carew, .333
1989: Kirby Puckett, .339

League Leaders in Home Runs
1962: Harmon Killebrew, 48
1963: Harmon Killebrew, 45
1964: Harmon Killebrew, 49
1967: Harmon Killebrew, 44
    (tie)

Rod Carew

Twenty-Game Winners
1962: Camilo Pascual, 20
1963: Camilo Pascual, 21
1965: Jim "Mudcat" Grant, 21
1966: Jim Kaat, 25
1967: Dean Chance, 20
1969: Jim Perry, 20
1969: Dave Boswell, 20
1970: Jim Perry, 24
1973: Bert Blyleven, 20
1977: Dave Goltz, 20
1979: Jerry Koosman, 20
1988: Frank Viola, 24
1991: Scott Erickson, 20
1997: Brad Radke, 20

Jim Kaat

No-Hitters
August 26, 1962: Jack Kralick vs. Kansas City Athletics
August 6, 1967: Dean Chance vs. Boston Red Sox (five-inning perfect game, stopped by rain)
August 25, 1967: Dean Chance vs. Cleveland Indians
April 27, 1994: Scott Erickson vs. Milwaukee Brewers
September 11, 1999: Eric Milton vs. Anaheim Angels

Dean Chance

Most Valuable Players
1965: Zoilo Versalles
1969: Harmon Killebrew
1977: Rod Carew

Cy Young Award Winners
1970: Jim Perry
1988: Frank Viola

*In 1997 major-league baseball decided that all teams would retire number 42 to honor Robinson for breaking baseball's color barrier in 1947.

Index

Cesar Tovar (top) provided a spark on offense and was versatile in the field. In 1968 Tovar played all nine defensive positions in one game. In 1973 Bert Blyleven (right) won 20 games and recorded a league-leading 9 shutouts. During another stint with the Twins, he helped them win the 1987 World Series. He ended his career as a Twin with a total of 29 shutouts—the most in team history. Since retiring, Blyleven has become a Twins broadcaster.